rose

pussy willow

pussy cat

soccer ball

toad

raccoon

drum

toadstool

horse

dragonfly

rabbit

bugle

nurse

patient

fox

beaver

witch

black cat

broom

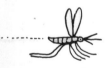

mosquito

HAMLYN

London • New York • Sydney • Toronto

moth

RICHARD SCARRY'S

BEST
WORD BOOK
EVER

mouse

moose

mushroom

moss

bear

paper aeroplane

CONTENTS

smashed

paper aeroplane

hoop

cat

First published 1964
Seventh impression 1970
Published by The Hamlyn Publishing Group Limited
London · New York · Sydney · Toronto
Hamlyn House, Feltham, Middlesex, England
for Golden Pleasure Books Ltd., by arrangement with
Western Publishing Company Inc.
Printed in Czechoslovakia by TSNP, Martin
T 1891
ISBN 0 601 07051 8

rabbit

log

frog

pig

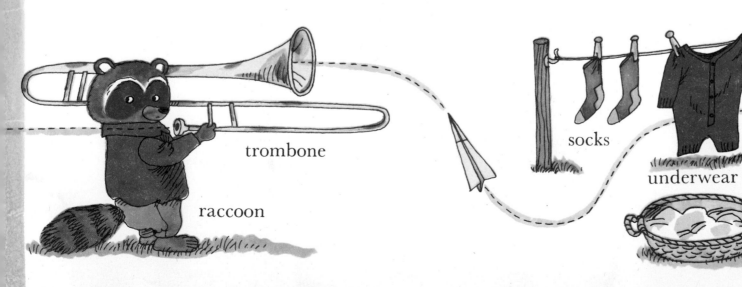

trombone

raccoon

socks

underwear

laundry basket

curtains

sun

window

THE NEW DAY

It is the morning of a new day.
The sun is shining.
Little Bear gets up out of bed.

face cloth

soap

towel

First he washes his
face and hands.

toothbrush

toothpaste

Then he brushes
his teeth.

comb

mirror

pyjamas

He combs his hair.

shirt

trousers

He dresses himself.

He makes his bed.

He comes promptly
when he is called to
breakfast.

8

Bear sits up straight in his chair.

He is very hungry. This is what he eats.

cold fruit juice

warm cereal

with cream

He doesn't eat the toaster.

pancakes

with butter and maple syrup

fried eggs

bacon

toast

muffins

honey

jam

hot cocoa

cool milk

and a waffle

When he finishes eating breakfast he helps his mother to wash and dry the dishes.

cup

saucer

plate

bowl

fork

knife

spoon

glass

jar

jug

frying pan

lid

pot

pan

bottle

juice squeezer

glass

Now he is ready to play with his friends.

9

THE RABBIT FAMILY'S HOUSE

Father Rabbit, Mother Rabbit, and the
Rabbit Brothers are getting ready for
the new day. Their friend Owl
is waiting for the two brothers
to come out to play.
Can you find him?

chimney

roof

mirror

father

lamp

bed

bedroom

cupboard

dining room

table

kitchen

sink

chair

floor

back door

stove

mother

axe

lawn

bird bath

woodpile

WHOO

owl

smoke

television
aerial

light
switch

television set

record player

bunk bed

bathroom

landing

boys' bedroom

front door

living room

candle

outside
light

picture

telephone

fireplace

stairs

sofa

front
hall

door mat

rug

window

stone path

11

AT THE PLAYGROUND

The children are all having fun doing different things. Which children are doing the things you like best?

see-saw

slide

leapfrog

somersault

hide-and-seek

ring-a-ring-o'-roses

skipping rope

ladder

rings

swing

sliding pole

top

roller skates

12

bubble blowing

kite

jungle gym

merry-go-round

tag

tossing the ring

hoop rolling

jacks

marbles

sand pit

kite string

bouncing ball

hopscotch

13

hammer

nail

TOOLS

Everyone is very busy
working with his tools.
Who always carries his
tool with him?
He has a red head.

chart pin

axe

carpenter

ladder

board

sandpaper

log

sawdust

hacksaw

drill

plane

woodpecker

jig saw

wood shavings

screwdriver

file

screws

pliers

14

bowsaw

trowel

bricklayer

hoe

brick

brick wall

cement

timber

fence painter

paint brush

ball of twine

saw horse

barrel

paint

tack

tack hammer

hatchet

ruler

folding ruler

tool box

jackknife

square

putty knife

shovel

bolt

nut

earth

compass

wheelbarrow

pick axe

monkey wrench

glue

15

crow

scarecrow

plough

field

tractor

weather vane

barn

goat

tin can

milk churn

hayloft

stall

pail

farm truck

cart

hen

cock

baby chick

pigsty

dog kennel

16

haystack

cow

apple tree

farmhouse

water pump

meadow

fence

sheep

horse

apple

grass

clothes-line

clothes basket

FARMER BEAR'S FARM

Farmer Bear has a very busy farm.
What is Mrs Bear doing? What is the horse doing?
What is the duck doing?
What is the scarecrow
supposed to be doing? He is
not doing it, is he?

FRESH
HONEY
AND
EGGS

chicken house

well

duck pond

duck   ducklings

bee

pitchfork

beehive

17

weather instruments

blimp

control tower

microphone

helicopter

AT THE AIRPORT

The man in the control tower is talking
into his microphone. He is talking to the
handsome pilot by radio. He is telling him
that he will have nice weather on his flight.

baggage train

waiting
room

binoculars

tourist

camera

observation deck

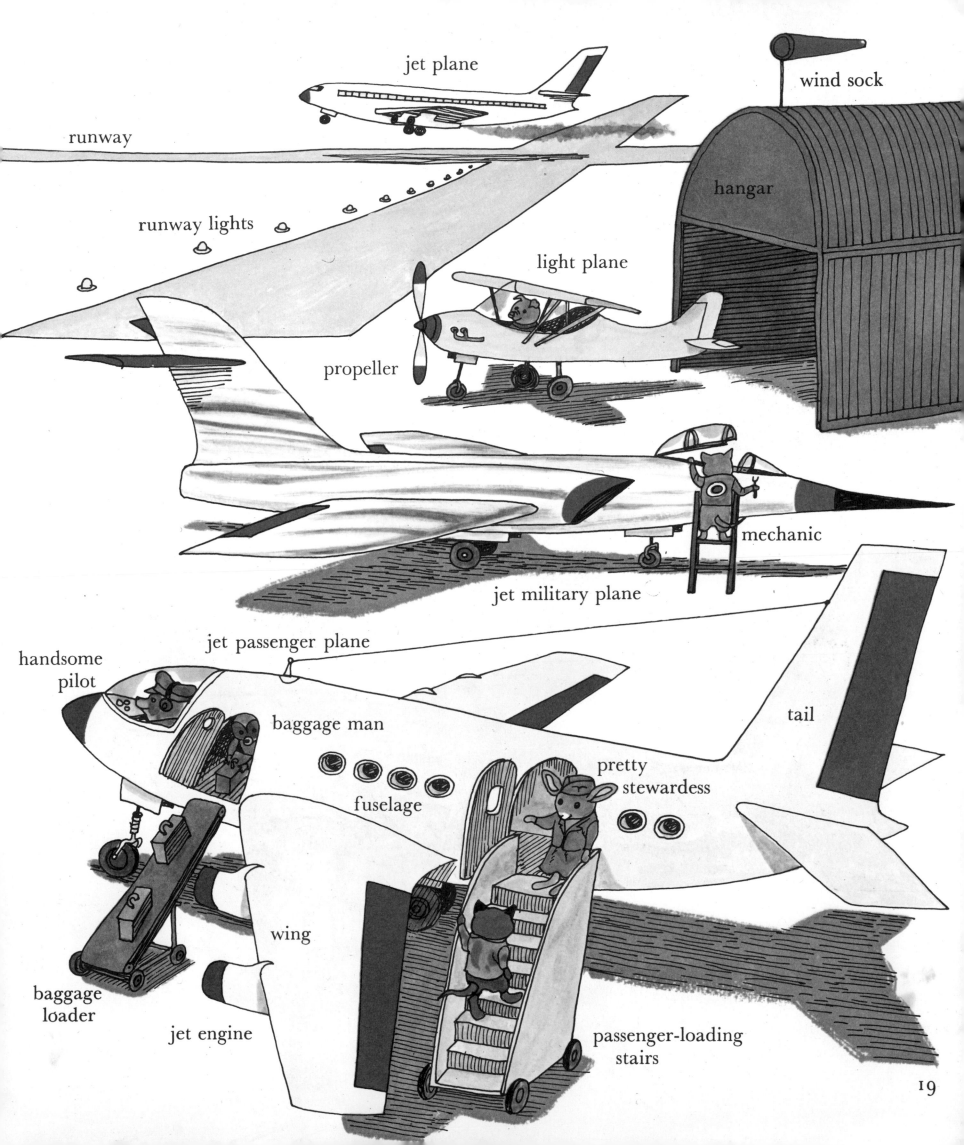

jet plane

wind sock

runway

hangar

runway lights

light plane

propeller

mechanic

jet military plane

jet passenger plane

handsome
pilot

baggage man

tail

fuselage

pretty
stewardess

wing

baggage
loader

jet engine

passenger-loading
stairs

19

TOYS

When you play with toys, it is more fun
if your share them with your friends.
When you play games you may win and
sometimes you may lose. Bear is a good sport.
He is losing a game but he might
win the next time.
Do you think he might
win the next game?

tricycle

teddy bear

electric trains

doll

blocks

lorry and loader

Bear is losing.

game

Rabbit is winning.

building set

20

castle

croquet

toy soldiers

tea set

robot

racing car

typewriter

bean bags

doll's house

rocking horse

scooter

glider

bow and arrow

21

IN THE FLOWER GARDEN

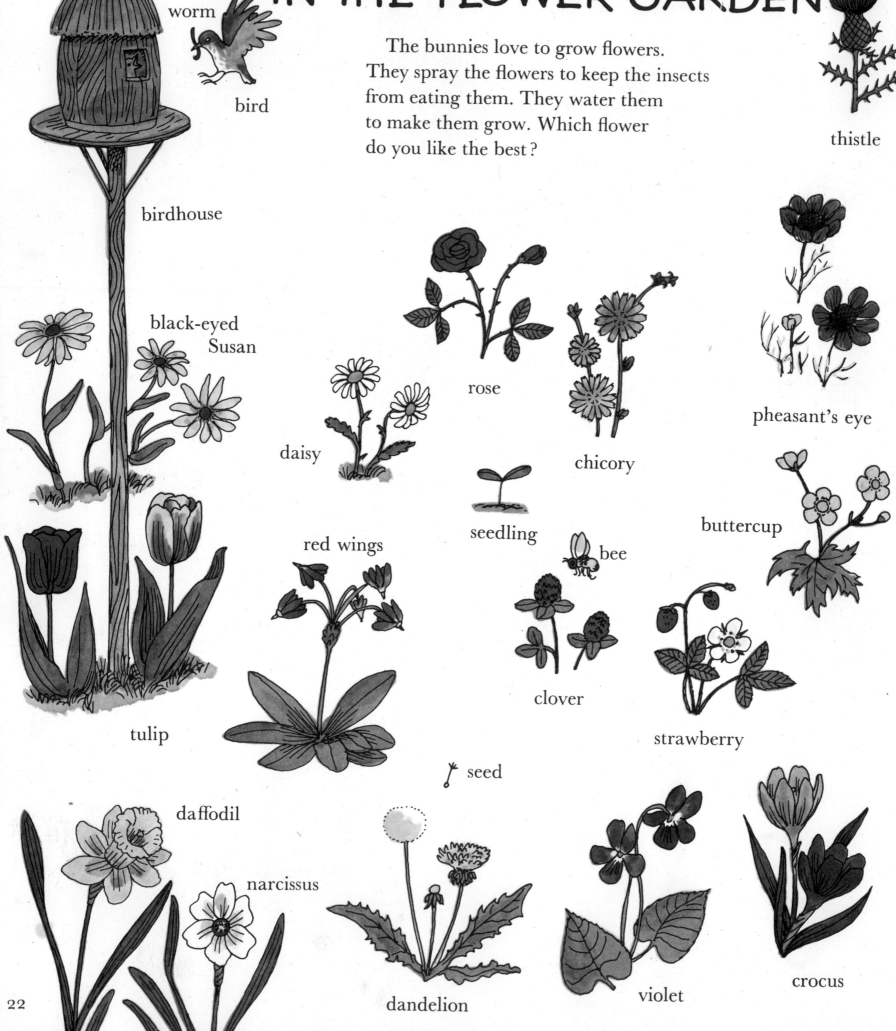

worm

bird

birdhouse

thistle

The bunnies love to grow flowers.
They spray the flowers to keep the insects
from eating them. They water them
to make them grow. Which flower
do you like the best?

black-eyed
Susan

rose

pheasant's eye

daisy

chicory

seedling

bee

buttercup

red wings

clover

strawberry

tulip

seed

daffodil

narcissus

dandelion

violet

crocus

morning-glory

sunflower

hollyhock

zinnia

foxglove

pink

tiger lily

forget-me-not

aster

insect-spray can

bellflower

bluebell

sweet william

petunia

pansy

beetle

poppy

flower basket

seed

watering can

trowel

seed packet

lily of the valley

flower pot

cultivator

bamboo rake

23

hook

saw

scales

ham

MEATS

wrapping paper

twine

meat cleaver

butcher

pickle barrel

bologna

frankfurters

hamburger

dustbin

bacon

chop

fish

steak

a piglet who wants
to be a butcher when
he grows up

cart

sawdust

AT THE SUPERMARKET

Mrs Pig is buying groceries for her family.
What would you like to buy the next time
you go to the market?
Would you like to buy a pickle?

books

GOLDEN PLEASURE BOOKS

customer

orange juice

raisins

money

handbag

cashier

yoghourt

eggs

butter

milk

cash register

24

FRUITS

pineapple

bananas

scales

grocer

apples

oranges

pears

grapefruit

melons

grapes

lemons

cherries

strawberries

raspberries

bilberries

plums

peaches

VEGETABLES

watermelon

coconut

cabbage

corn

beans

lettuce

tomatoes

asparagus

peas

spinach

potatoes

celery

beets

onions

cauliflower

carrots

cucumbers

turnip

biscuits

sugar

cereal

spaghetti

tinned food

peanut butter

broom

cheese

salt

apricots

baby food

bread

jam

25

MEALTIME

Father Pig, Mother Pig, and Peter Pig love to eat. There is so much food on the table it is hard to find Peter. Can you find him?

carving knife and fork

roast beef

meat dish

tablespoon

coffee pot

teapot

salt cellar

pepper pot

fork

dinner plate

glass

cream jug

cup

knife

saucer

spoon

napkin

sugar bowl

turkey

cake

milk jug

baked potatoes

green beans

blancmange

mashed swede

cranberry jelly

beetroots

onions

mashed potatoes

ice cream

butter

steak

peas

soup

pie

salad

rye bread

white bread

rolls

27

smokestack

submarine

stern

ocean liner

bow

tug

police boat

barge

ferry boat

pirate ship

BOATS AND SHIPS

What do you see in the water which is not
a boat? It helps boats find
the place they want to go.

motor boat

paddle

canoe

28

kayak

oar   rowing boat

freighter

lightship

AMBROSE

CG-7

launch

oil tanker

fireboat

fishing
nets

sport fishing-boat

fishing trawler

speedboat

IO

houseboat

raft

GRETEL

yacht

lightbuoy

2

29

KEEPING HEALTHY

Your doctor and your dentist are two of your very best friends. They want to help you to stay strong, healthy, and happy. Will you give your doctor and dentist a great big smile the next time you see them? How big can you smile?

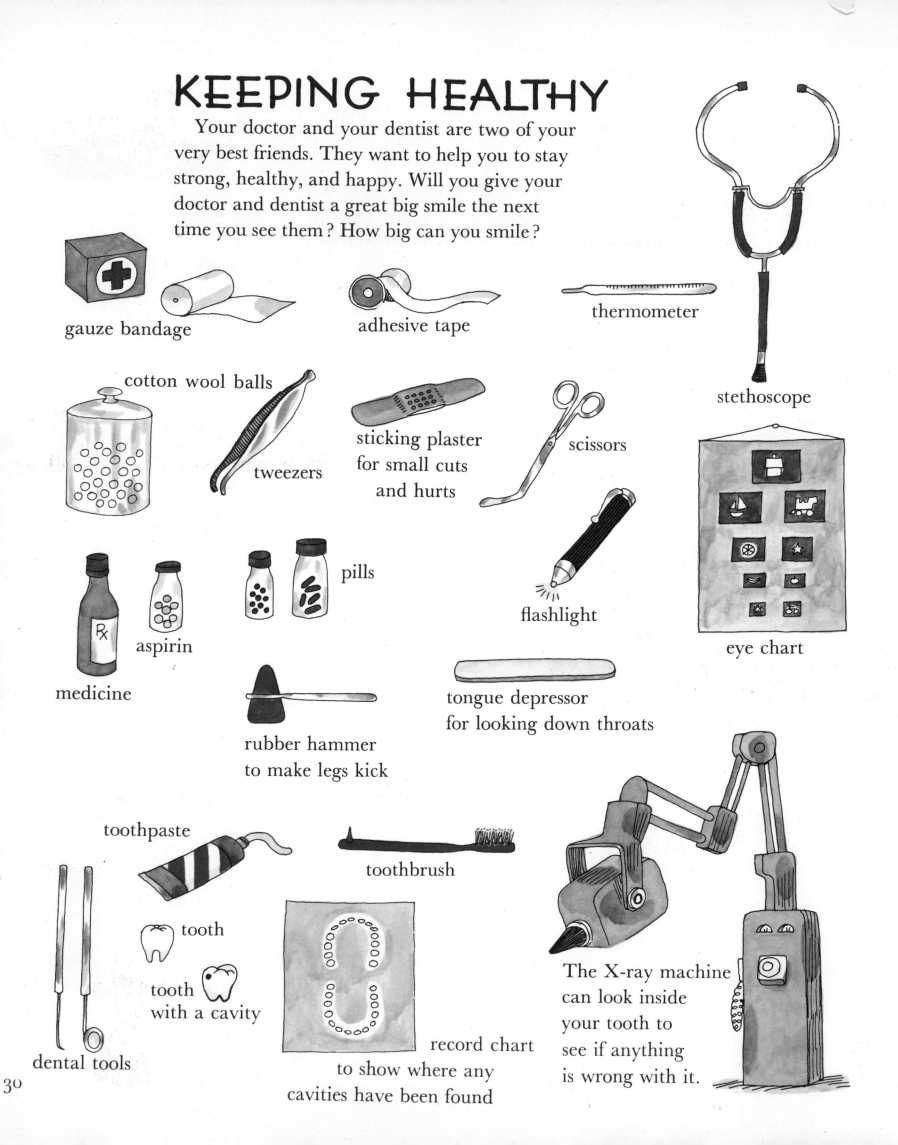

gauze bandage

adhesive tape

thermometer

stethoscope

cotton wool balls

tweezers

sticking plaster
for small cuts
and hurts

scissors

flashlight

eye chart

pills

aspirin

medicine

rubber hammer
to make legs kick

tongue depressor
for looking down throats

toothpaste

toothbrush

tooth

tooth
with a cavity

dental tools

record chart
to show where any
cavities have been found

The X-ray machine
can look inside
your tooth to
see if anything
is wrong with it.

At the doctor's surgery

nurse

test tube

scales

hurt tail

patient   doctor

dental
drill

At the dentist's surgery

dentist

mouth-rinse
bowl

instrument table
water cup

dental unit

dentist's chair

dental nurse

The dental nurse hasn't a cavity in her teeth.
Brush your teeth well and you may not get any.

31

THE BEAR TWINS GET DRESSED

Brother Bear woke up one cold, frosty morning.
He wanted to dress very warmly before
he went outside.

He yawned and got up out of bed.

He took off his pyjamas
and left them on the floor.
Naughty bear!

slippers

pyjama top

pyjama bottom

He put on his

underwear

cap

shirt

trousers

overalls

tie

sweater

socks

hat

muffler

plimsolls

gloves

jacket

overcoat

raincoat

and sou'wester

As he was walking out of the front door
his Mother said, 'Don't forget
to put your boots on!'

boots

32

Sister Bear got up out of bed.

She took off her pretty nightgown and put it away neatly. Nice bear!

nightgown

She put on her

panties

petticoat

hair ribbon

blouse

skirt

pinafore

stockings

ear muffs

shoes

snow suit

and mittens.

She put her handkerchief

and purse

in her handbag

As she was walking out of the front door her mother said, 'Don't forget to put your boots on!'

Do you ever forget to put on your boots?

33

deer

lion

elephant

tiger

panda

monkeys

brown bear

gorilla

polar bear

34

buffalo

camel

zebra

zoo keeper

giraffe

sealion

leopard

zoo train

AT THE ZOO

Mr and Mrs Mouse took
their children to the zoo.
How will those children
ever be able to get
all those balloons
into their house tonight?
Which is your favourite animal
at the zoo?

rhinoceros

hippopotamus

DRAWING AND PAINTING

Everyone likes to draw and paint. Can you draw a ferris wheel? They are fun to ride on and they are fun to draw.

make orange

make green

make grey

ferris wheel

make violet

make pink

make brown

water dish

paint brushes

poster paint

rubber

paint box

pens

ink

crayons

pastels

pencil

36

mural painting

artist

dinosaur

scaffold

pastel sketch

canvas

still-life model

pad of paper

life model

oil painting

palette

smock

watercolour painting

finger painting

paper

pencil drawing

NUMBERS

How high can you count?
Can you count up to
twenty ladybirds?
I'll bet you can.

1 one whale

2 two walruses

3 three piggy banks

4 four bells

5 five grasshoppers

6 six eggs

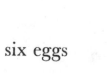

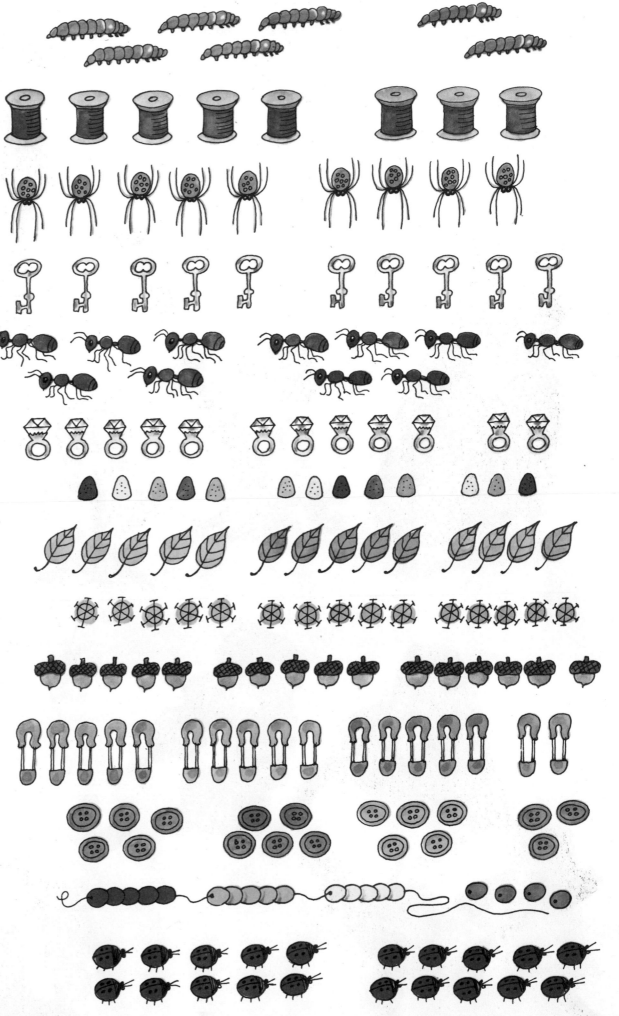

7	seven caterpillars
8	eight reels
9	nine spiders
10	ten keys
11	eleven ants
12	twelve rings
13	thirteen sweets
14	fourteen leaves
15	fifteen snowflakes
16	sixteen acorns
17	seventeen pins
18	eighteen buttons
19	nineteen beads
20	twenty ladybirds

MUSIC MAKING

The conductor leads the orchestra by waving his baton. The musicians are playing a very gay tune.
Which of the musical instruments do you think you could learn to play?

bassoon

double bass

cello

oboe

clarinet

flute

piccolo

violin

baton

viola

conductor

piano

podium

notes

kettle drums

snare drum

bass drum

cymbals

triangle

saxophone

French horn

trumpet

tuba

tambourine

cornet

trombone

banjo

guitar

harp

accordion

harmonica

comb and tissue paper

41

BOOK PUBLISHER

editor

COSTUMES

NEWSPAPER OFFICE

Dancing School

Book Shop

CHEMIST

book reader

skyscraper

aerial

church

flats

traffic lights

telephone box

van

street

IN THE CITY

Mouse has just bought a book at the book shop.
He is going to buy a newspaper and then join
his rabbit friends at the café and drink some
lemonade with them. Show with your finger the way
he will go. Remember to make him look both
ways before he crosses a street.

42

hotel

street sign

park

park bench

statue

RESTAURANT

manhole

DANGER

one way

taxi

barber's shop

café

delivery man

police car

TAXI

THEATRE

NOW PLAYING

Mis

CA

bus

pavement

underground entrance

newspapers

newsagent

underground station

43

radio tower

A DRIVE
IN THE COUNTRY

There are many things to see when
you take a drive in the country.
Can you see what the mountain climber
has dropped out of his knapsack?

ocean

island

factory

petrol
station

lake

tunnel

petrol pump

toll gate

motorway

bridge

farm

brook

mill

stream

waterfall

44

layby

picnickers

lighthouse

fire lookout tower

beach

bay

crane

drawbridge

woods

harbour

hill

mountain

village

tug

windmill

river

pond

log cabin

road

mountain climber

forest

knapsack

cliff

apple

45

HOLIDAYS

Which holiday do you like best?
I bet you like them all.
Holidays are always very happy times,
aren't they? What did you get from
Santa Claus last Christmas?

horn

New Year's Day

valentine

St Valentine's Day

balloons

rattle

Easter

Easter egg

Easter bunny

Easter chick

cake   ice cream

Birthday

Carnival procession

fireworks

bugle

trumpet

bass drum

fife

drum

uniform

46

ghost

Hallowe'en

moon

skeleton

black cat

witch's broom

candle

wreath

holly

Christmas

angel

Christmas tree

ornaments

tree lights

stockings

beard

fireplace

Santa Claus

bag

present

47

AT SCHOOL

School is fun. There are so many things we learn to do. Little Bear is learning how to find a lost glove.

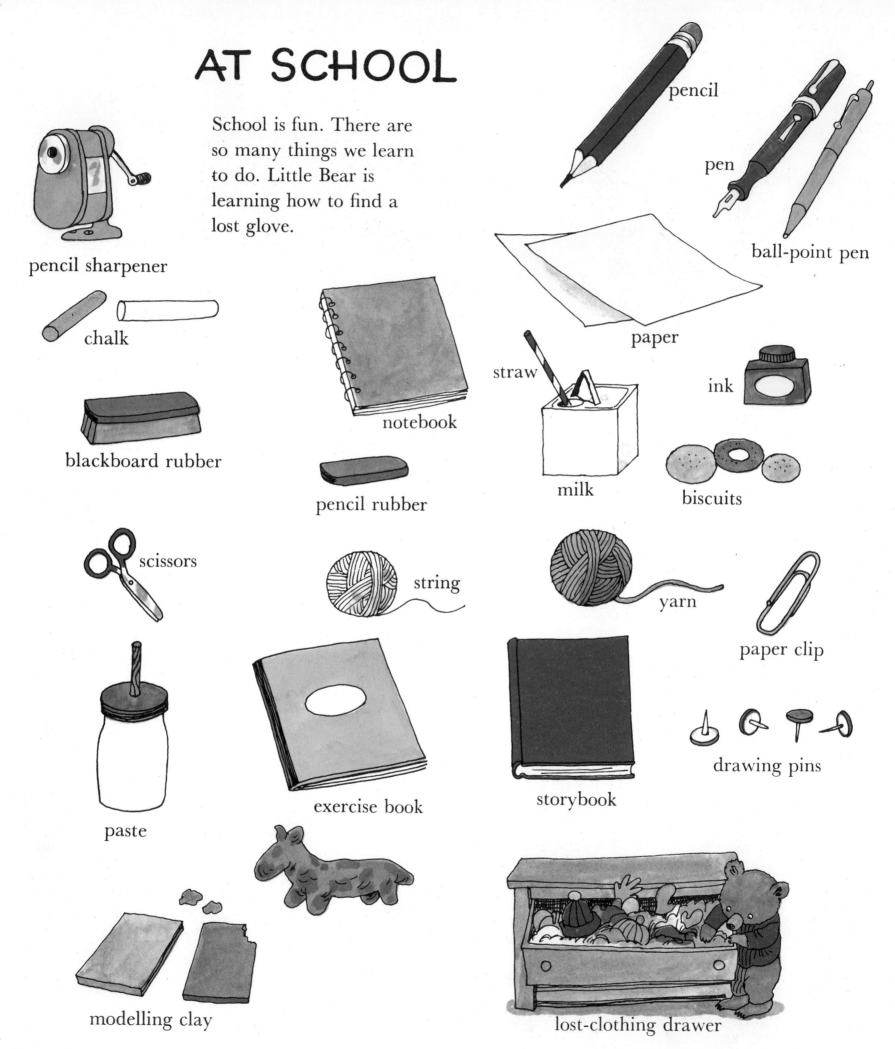

pencil sharpener

pencil

pen

ball-point pen

chalk

blackboard rubber

notebook

pencil rubber

paper

straw

ink

milk

biscuits

scissors

string

yarn

paper clip

paste

exercise book

storybook

drawing pins

modelling clay

lost-clothing drawer

48

clock

bell

blackboard

calendar

teacher

JANUARY

a b c

cat dog

map

map stand

inkwell

waste-paper basket

artist

pupil

desk

classroom

paper dolls

headmaster

49

refrigerator

kitchen cabinet

door knob

tin opener

soap

teapot

light socket

work surface

freezer

refuse bin

clothes-washer

dish-washer

egg beater

laundry basket

stool

spoon

measuring jug

egg shells

mixing bowl

rolling pin

biscuit cutter

dough

strainer

cake tin

funnel

baking tray

sauce bottle

slice

mincer

flour bin

sugar bowl

mustard pot

broom cupboard

feather duster

broom

mop

dust pan

vacuum cleaner

shelf

egg timer

fly swatter

hood

coffee pot

burner

kettle

stove

oven

iron

ironing board

IN THE KITCHEN

All the little piglets like to help their mother in the kitchen. They are making good things to eat. What is Mother Pig putting into the oven?

teaspoon

tablespoon

soupspoon

double boiler

blender

pestle

toaster

mortar

saucepan

corkscrew

ladle

colander

cutting board

measuring spoons

matches

potato masher

salt cellar

pepper mill

electric mixer

cookery book

carving fork and knife

51

BUILDINGS

Buildings are used for different things. You wouldn't kick a ball in a museum or a cathedral. Where is a good place to kick a football?
What do people do in the other buildings?

skyscraper

fort

tower

museum

arch

school

pyramid

football

stadium

windmill

mosque

cathedral

church

library

factory

53

WHEN YOU GROW UP

What would you like to be when you are bigger? Would you like to be a good cook like your father? Or would you like to be a doctor or a nurse?

What would you like to be?

policeman

fireman

sailor

nurse

milkman

farmer

doctor

carpenter

musician

cowboy

butcher

dentist

secretary

good cook

54

singer

artist

pilot

fisherman

lorry driver

teacher

garage mechanic

ticket inspector

train passenger

shopkeeper

soldier

librarian

dancer

daddy

mummy

55

THE ALPHABET

The alligator is eating an apple.
The goose is wearing gloves.
What is the xiphias doing?

A alligator

B bear

C cat

D dog

E egg

F fish

G goose

H heart

I ice cream

J jug

K kangaroo

L letter

M mouse

N nut

O owl

P present

Q queen

R rug

S spider

T tortoise

U umbrella

V vase

W walrus

X xiphias

Y yarn

Z zip

THINGS WE DO

There are many things
that we can do. And there
are some things we cannot do.
What is one thing we can't do?
Look and see.

dig

blow

build

break

sleep

wake up

walk

run

stand

sit

read

watch

draw and write

58

pull

push

kick

talk

listen

shout

whisper

eat

laugh

smile

cry

drink

jump over

crawl under

fall down

we can't fly

peep

raise a hat

go up

go down

go in

come out

WORK MACHINES

Busy, busy, busy bears. Most of the bears are busy moving earth with their machines. But there is one bear who has a machine which does something else to the earth. Which one is it? What is he doing?

bulldozer

earth

excavator

dump trailer

60

tractor scraper

dump truck

tractor shovel

bucket loader

earth

roller

smooth earth

and tractor

rough earth

61

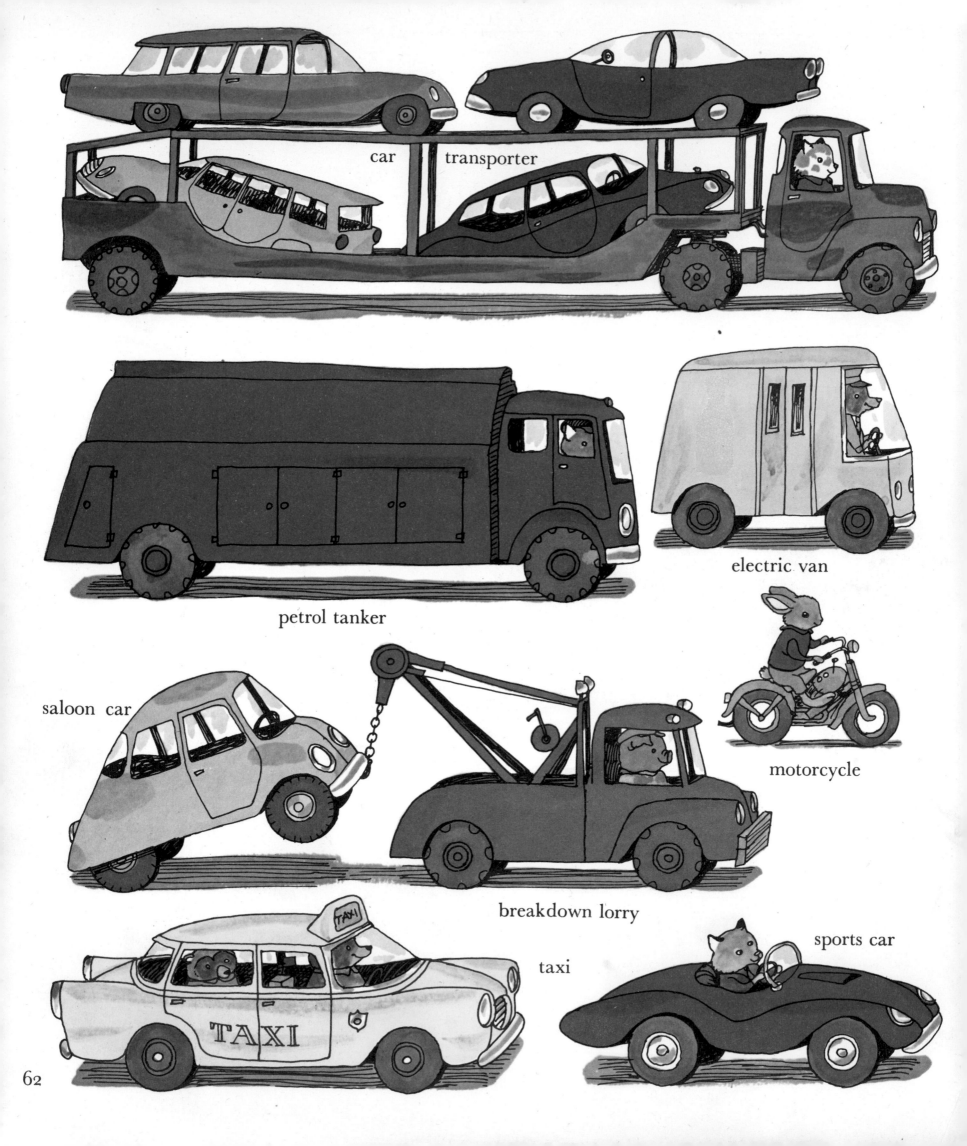

car transporter

petrol tanker

electric van

saloon car

motorcycle

breakdown lorry

taxi

sports car

TAXI

62

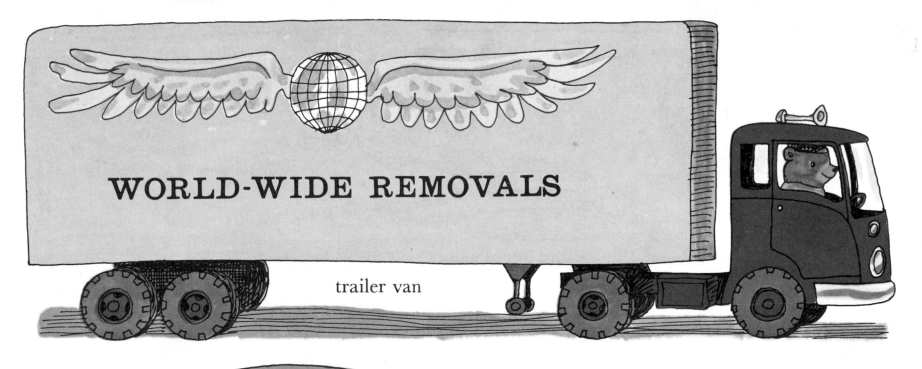

WORLD-WIDE REMOVALS

trailer van

CARS AND LORRIES

Down the street go the
cars and lorries.
But look! Some of the
cars don't have drivers.
Which cars have no drivers?

dustcart

boat trailer

station wagon

motor scooter

vintage car

SCHOOL BUS

school bus

HOTEL

GENERAL STORE

COWBOY SUITS

BANK

TOWN HALL

BOOTS

street lamp

hitching post

gold miner

burro

money box

cowboy

sheriff

headlight

frontier locomotive

stagecoach

wheel

BUFFALO BILL

cowcatcher

OUT WEST

Indian is coming to town to buy
a horse for his squaw to ride.
Why do you think it
would be nice for her to
have a horse to ride?

covered wagon

dust

BLACKSMITH

saddle

oxen

horseshoe

Indian

papoose

squaw

HAY FEED AND GRAIN

barrel

lasso

cattle truck

tender

cattle

corral

cowpony

65

round

square

triangle

diamond

star

crescent

heart

straight

curved

SHAPES AND SIZES

cone

thin

tall

big

short

fat

long

little

tiny

short

father

mother

THE BABY

That cat family has a new baby kitten.
They don't know what to name it.
What would you like
to name the new baby?
Write the kitten's name here.

—— —— —— —— —— ——

uncle

grandmother

rattle

baby

bottle

nappy

brother

sister

aunt

grandfather

playpen

cousin

high chair

cot

pushchair

cradle

play table

walker

pram

67

AT THE CIRCUS

The band is playing and the animals are doing their acts. What do you like to watch best at the circus?

tent pole

balancing pole

tightrope performer

tightrope

band

bareback rider

rope ladder

bandstand

circus horse

performing elephant

sawdust

ring

ringmaster

performing dog

clown

pennant

circus tent

trapeze

trapeze artist

acrobat

safety net

ticket seller

hoop

lion

whip

cage

lion tamer

juggler

trained sealion

balloon man

popcorn man

69

SPORTS

cricket ball

bat

wicket keeper

cap

fielder

stumps   pads

cricket

goalkeeper

referee

goal

whistle

football

dashing centre-forward

70

racquet

cabbage

net

tennis

gym slip

shorts

hockey

basket ball

table tennis

handle
bars

judge

cycle racing

71

TRAINS

Which train do you think
would be the most fun to run?
Would it be a goods train
or a passenger train?

signal

lantern

hand trolley

guard's van

flatbed

dining car

railway station

platform

luggage trolley

guard

72

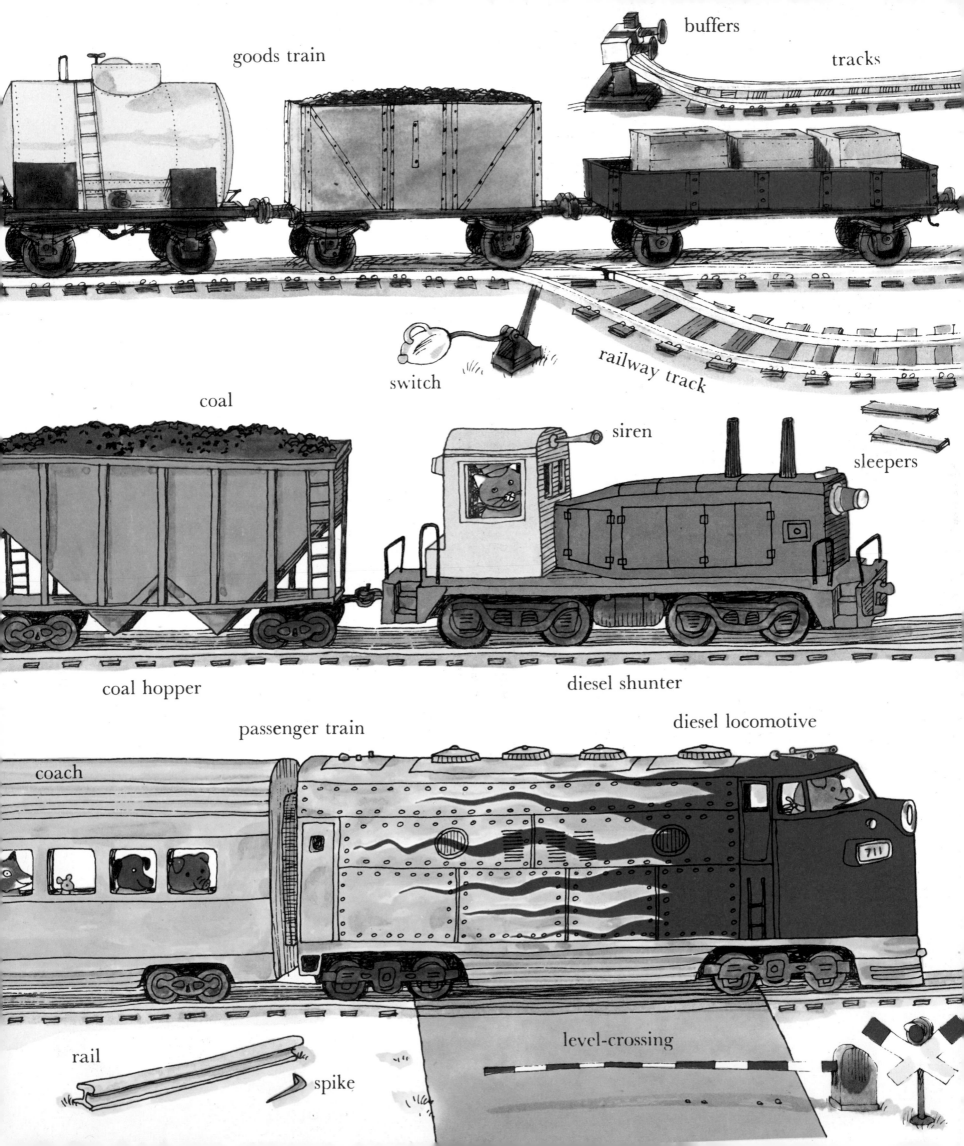

goods train

buffers

tracks

switch

railway track

coal

sleepers

siren

coal hopper

diesel shunter

diesel locomotive

passenger train

coach

711

rail

spike

level-crossing

BIRDS

Most birds can fly. Some birds can't fly.
One bird who can't fly lives at the South Pole.
He likes to slide on the ice. Which bird is it?

eagle

hawk

hummingbird

barn swallow

heron

cock

hen

chick

nuthatch

goose

pigeon

woodpeckers

duck

spoonbill

swan

duckling

flamingo

bittern

penguin

pelican

74

vulture

parrot

crow

owl

toucan

ground dove

puffin

robin

cardinal

jay

sparrow

wren

bluebird

sea gull

sandpiper

tern

canary

bird house

bird cage

nest

baby birds

ostrich

quail

pheasant

egret

stork

woodcock

ostrich egg

75

AT THE BEACH

In the summertime it is fun
to go to the beach.
What do you think
Rabbit hears in the seashell?
Is it the sound of the waves?

telescope

lighthouse

summer cottage

anchor

oar

beach toy

spade

rowing boat

sandpiper

sand castle

skate

mackerel

oyster

lobster

sea purse

clam

hermit crab

scallop

umbrella

sea gull

sun

shelter

flag pole

sand dune

boardwalk

lifeguard

beach grass

stairs

bathing house

beach chair

sea shell

starfish

sand dugout

waves

prawn

sprat

horseshoe crab

crab

flounder

seaweed

mussel

77

igloo

HOUSES

In different parts of the world
people live in different kinds of houses.
If you were invited to visit one of these houses,
which would you like to stay in?

tree house

stone house

mud hut

stilt house

grass house

desert tent

wooden frame house

felt tent

78

castle

half-timbered house

thatched-roof cottage

adobe house with tile roof

chalet

brick house

block of flats

houseboat

modern house

79

MAKING THINGS GROW

Everyone is working in the garden.
Mr Crow has a seed in his mouth.
Do you think he will plant it?
Or will he eat it?

water main

nozzle

hose

maize

gardener

spade

string

hoe

tomato
plants

seed row

seeds

seedlings

handle

rake

stake

garden fork

BEETS

TOMATOES

stones

fertiliser trolley

THE WEATHER

sun

cloud

When we go outdoors we see what the weather is like. Sometimes it is sunny. Sometimes it is cloudy. It can be windy, or cold, or hot. It can be snowing or raining. What was the weather like outdoors today?

lightning

rain

snowflakes

thermometer

hailstones

rainbow

windmill

wind

hat

rain drops

toad

foxtail grass

toadstool

a cat chasing a hat

ladybird

puddle

mud

81

CLEANING-UP TIME

Each of the animals has a job to do to make everything tidy around the house. What do you think each animal is about to do?

mop

cleaning powder

glue

sponge

spilled water

coat hanger

waste paper

wrench

eyeglasses

bag of nails

octopus who sews

hammer

torn bed-sheet

sewing machine

muddy boots

footprints

chipped vase

chip

paw prints on the wall

clothes rail

wire coat hangers

broken table leg

leaking tap

brush

dust pan

wastepaper-basket

fireplace ashes

bookcase

book

old newspapers

old magazines

wire coat hangers

Don't you think some of them should be thrown in the dustbin?

dustbin

kite

rain shower

plough

bird

nest

buds

tree

SPRING

Look at that baby lamb hop!
It is spring. He is happy.
Look at Mr Bear coming out of
his cave! It is spring.
Now he can use his new
lawn mower.

lamb

bush

bridge

brook

cave

fern

tortoise

roots

pussy willow

daffodil

violets

lawn mower

crocus

84

cow

meadow

calf

cornfield

fence

SUMMER

Do you like to go
on picnics in the summer time?
Ants just love to go to picnics.
Do you know why?

station wagon

tent

fly

camp bed

screen

cooking grill

water carrier

charcoal

picnic basket

hamburger

mosquito

fishing rod

charcoal bag

hotdog

gherkin

paper cup

mustard

ketchup

rock

ants

float

landing stage

bulrushes

pond

frog

water lily

dragonfly

pebbles

stones

85

sun

pheasant

falling leaves

gate

stone wall

grouse

nuts

roadside stand

maize cobs

cider

jam

AUTUMN

In the autumn the air gets colder. The green leaves turn to bright colours. Then they fall to the ground. Who is raking them all up?

smoke

basket of apples

flames

turkey

rake

bonfire

86

leaves

snowstorm

WINTER

There are many ways to have fun on the snow and ice. Maybe you would like to do all of them. Would you?

sleigh

icicle

fishing hut

skis

sledge

toboggan

ice fishing

ice-skating rink

snowball

hockey stick

puck

ice skates

muffler

spare tyre

jeep

snowplough

a pig all wrapped up

pipe

snowman

87

LITTLE THINGS

Here are many little things.
What little thing do you sometimes
put on your Mummy's wall?

worm

dandelion seed

button

reel

thread

fly

ant

drop of water

ladybird

bead

snowflake

pin

fingerprint

petal

mosquito

butterfly

fish-hook

crumb

bubble

peanut

tack

pen nib

tea leaf

sweet

pea

caterpillar

jelly bean

firefly

ring

sand

bilberry

moth

rice

tadpole

keyhole

shell

marble

blade of grass

paper clip

cricket

raisin

beetle

raspberry

thimble

pincushion

hermit crab

pebble

sea horse

bee

mushroom

pearl

ink spot

confetti

feather

splinter

bean

safety pin

baby mouse

dot

88

PARTS OF THE BODY

Bear picks things up in his paws.
What do you pick things up with?

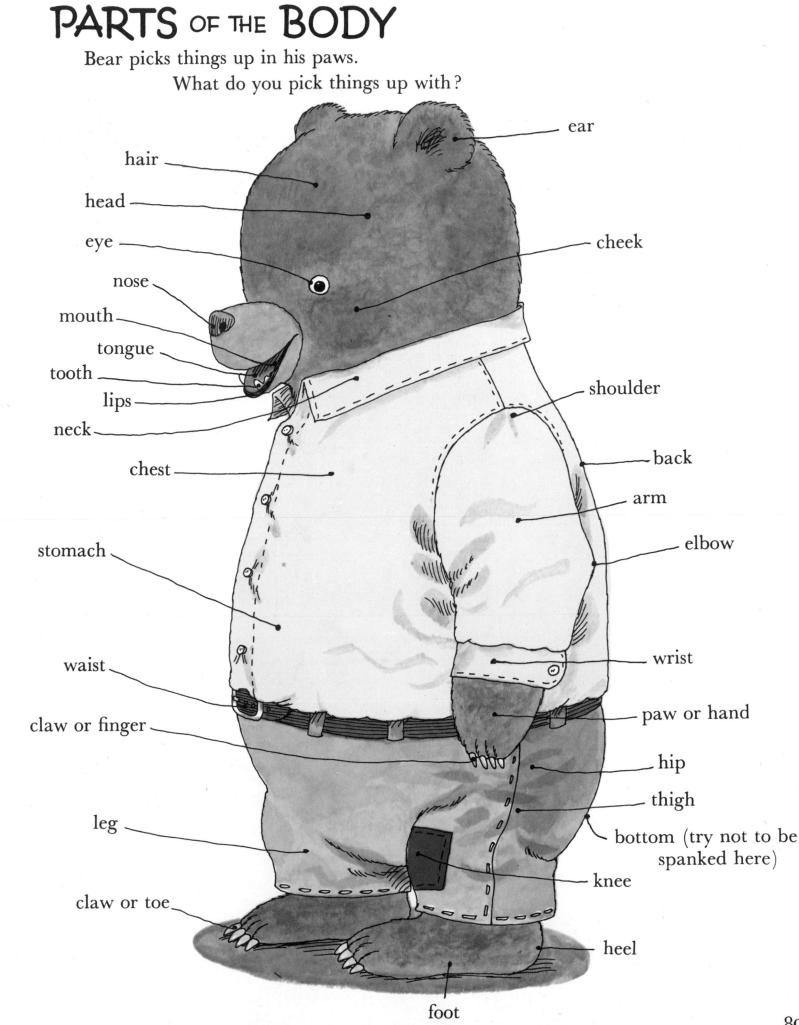

ear

hair

head

eye

cheek

nose

mouth

tongue

tooth

shoulder

lips

neck

back

chest

arm

elbow

stomach

waist

wrist

claw or finger

paw or hand

hip

thigh

leg

bottom (try not to be
spanked here)

knee

claw or toe

heel

foot

BEDTIME

Who is that hiding under the bed?
Find the naughty rascal and tell him to brush his
teeth and get into bed.

shower

medicine
cabinet

brush

curtain

tap

soap suds

washbasin

bath

towel

bath mat

slippers

water closet

the bathroom

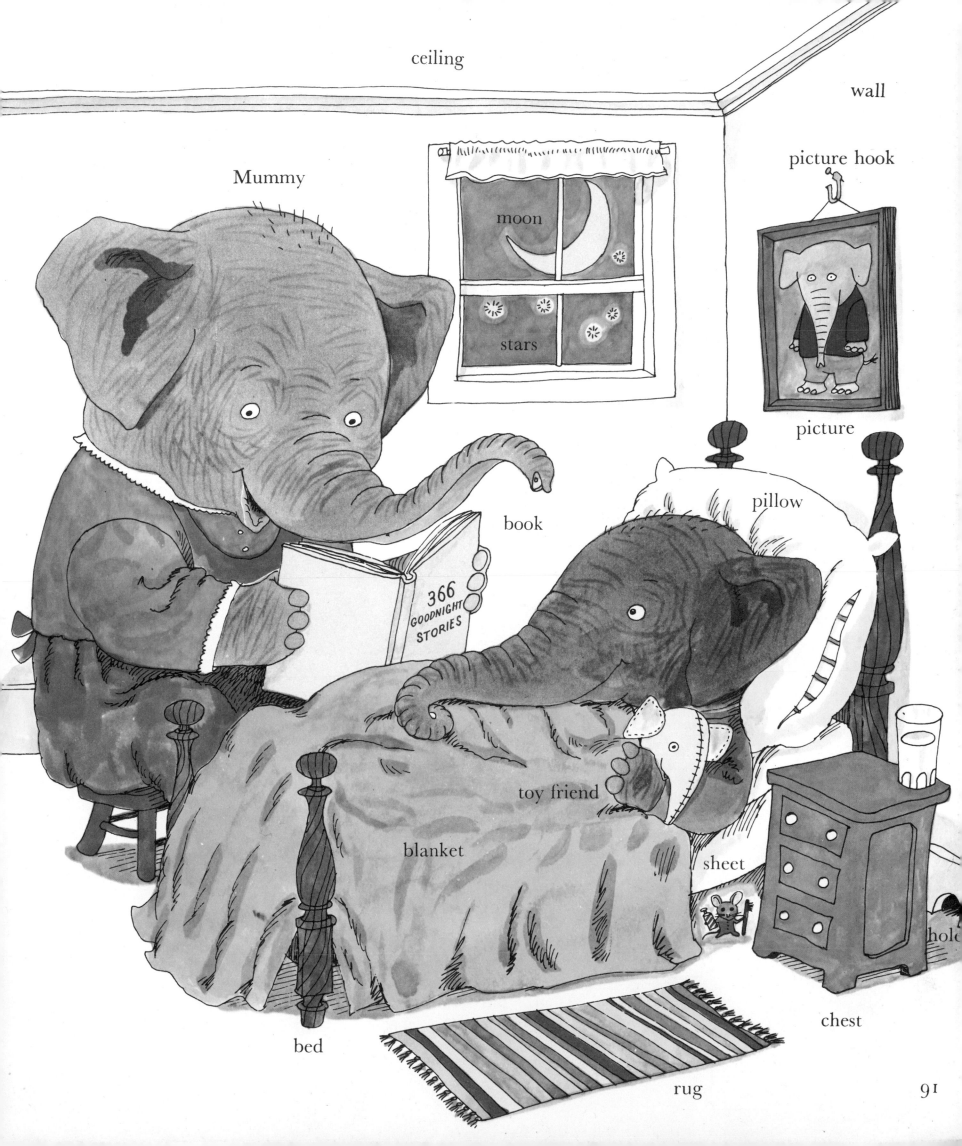

ceiling

wall

picture hook

Mummy

moon

stars

picture

book

pillow

366 GOODNIGHT STORIES

toy friend

blanket

sheet

chest

bed

rug

hole

91

THE LAST WORDS OF THE DAY

The animals have a last word to say
before they go to bed.

cheep

oink

bow-wow

meow

cut-cut

gruff

sniff-sniff

yipe

quack

squeek

whoo

chug-a-room

Do you know what they are saying?
They are saying 'Good night'.

galumpf, galumpf, galumpf

Walrus has some last words, too.
Do you know what he is saying?

cock

hen

baby chick

mole

letter

guitarist

crow

spade

rabbit

fly

pig

mouse

umbrella

vase

walrus

lamb

Sir Winston
London
England